BEING FEMALE **IN AMERICA**

# SEXISM AND RACE

BY DUCHESS HARRIS, JD, PHD
WITH NADINE PINEDE, PHD

**Essential Library**

An Imprint of Abdo Publishing | abdopublishing.com

# ABDOPUBLISHING.COM

Published by Abdo Publishing, a division of ABDO, PO Box 398166, Minneapolis, Minnesota 55439. Copyright © 2018 by Abdo Consulting Group, Inc. International copyrights reserved in all countries. No part of this book may be reproduced in any form without written permission from the publisher. Essential Library™ is a trademark and logo of Abdo Publishing.

Printed in the United States of America, North Mankato, Minnesota
092017
012018

**THIS BOOK CONTAINS RECYCLED MATERIALS**

Cover Photo: Yulia Buchatskaya/Shutterstock Images
Interior Photos: Ann Hermes/The Christian Science Monitor/AP Images, 4–5; Jean-Philippe Ksiazek/AFP/Getty Images, 8–9; Charles Sykes/Invision/AP Images, 11; Rachel Worth/Wenn Photos/Newscom, 13; MPI/Archive Photos/Getty Images, 16–17; Afro American Newspapers/Gado/Archive Photos/Getty Images, 19; Jorg Carstensen/dpa/picture-alliance/Newscom, 22; Hulton Archive/Getty Images, 26–27; Arnold Genthe/Underwood Archives/Archive Photos/Getty Images, 29; Bettmann/Getty Images, 34–35, 50–51; Jae C. Hong/AP Images, 38–39; Jacquelyn Martin/AP Images, 42–43; Red Line Editorial, 46; AP Images, 52–53, 68; Robert Kneschke/Shutterstock Images, 58; Monkey Business Images/Shutterstock Images, 62–63; J.P. Moczulski/The Canadian Press/AP Images, 70; George Bridges/AP Images, 72–73; Pablo Martinez Monsivais/AP Images, 77; Jordan Strauss/Invision for Producers Guild of America/AP Images, 82; J. Scott Applewhite/AP Images, 84–85; Jose Luis Magana/AP Images, 86; Angela Weiss/AFP/Getty Images, 88–89; Janette Pellegrini/Getty Images for Girls Write Now/Getty Images Entertainment/Getty Images, 91; John Springer Collection/Corbis Historical/Getty Images, 94

Editor: Arnold Ringstad
Series Designer: Maggie Villaume

## PUBLISHER'S CATALOGING-IN-PUBLICATION DATA

Names: Harris, Duchess, author | Pinede, Nadine, author.
Title: Sexism and race / by Duchess Harris and Nadine Pinede.
Description: Minneapolis, Minnesota : Abdo Publishing, 2018. | Series: Being female in America |
Identifiers: LCCN 2017946732 | ISBN 9781532113086 (lib.bdg.) | ISBN 9781532151965 (ebook)
Subjects: LCSH: Sexism--Juvenile literature. | Race discrimination--Juvenile literature. | Social history--Juvenile literature.
Classification: DDC 305.0--dc23
LC record available at https://lccn.loc.gov/2017946732

# CONTENTS

# THE MARCH HEARD
# AROUND THE WORLD

The Women's March on Washington began as a small protest suggested by two people on Facebook. Before it was over, it became the single largest day of protest in US history. On Saturday, January 21, 2017, nearly five million people took part in demonstrations that ranged from a handful in small towns to crowds of hundreds of thousands in major cities around the world.[1]

## THE WOMEN'S MARCH BY THE NUMBERS

It has been a challenge to measure the exact number of participants in the Women's Marches around the world, but these are best estimates:

- 1 in 100 people in the United States marched, totaling at least 3.3 million[2]

- 500,000 marchers in Washington, DC

- 250,000 in Chicago, Illinois

- 200,000 in Los Angeles, California

- 100,000 in the United Kingdom

- 673 marches in 100 cities in 60 countries on 7 continents, including Antarctica[3]

In Berlin, Germany, they stood before the Brandenburg Gate, a symbol of European unity. In Paris, France, they protested in front of the Eiffel Tower. They gathered from Antarctica to Zimbabwe. In Washington, DC, alone, more than three times the number of people participated in the march than attended the presidential inauguration the previous day.

It had been a contentious presidential campaign. The first female presidential candidate from a major party, Hillary Clinton, had run against businessman and reality-television star Donald Trump. Trump had upset many people with a history of words and actions they felt were sexist. But he won the election on the night of November 8, 2016. On the day after his January 20 inauguration, women and men across the globe came together in cities around the world. One woman said she came to the march "because I have a daughter." Another said she came "to be counted," not to protest against anything: "It's about healing." Others said they wanted to "unite under a message of inclusivity, progress, and love" and to protest "hatred, racism, divisiveness, homophobia, misogyny, xenophobia, and ignorance." White women held signs that said "Black Lives Matter."[4]

Despite this show of unity on a wide array of social justice issues, a troubling source of conflict had simmered in the months leading up to the march. An impassioned post on social media by a 27-year-old African-American woman blogger on December 28 led some white women to decide they would not be welcome at the Women's March on Washington and they would not participate. The blogger, ShiShi Rose, had suggested that white women should do more listening and less talking. She criticized those who turned to activism only after Trump's election. With such conflicts, the Women's March

Protesters in France joined their counterparts across the world in speaking out about social justice.

exposed some of the dividing lines of race and class that had always existed in the women's movement.

## SOCIAL MEDIA AND THE MARCH

To understand these lines, it's helpful to know the backstory. The idea for the Women's March came from Teresa Shook, a retired lawyer living in Hawaii who proposed a protest on Facebook the night after the presidential election. When she woke up the next day, more than 10,000 people had stated they would attend. In New York, the fashion designer Bob Bland, creator of the "Nasty Woman" T-shirt inspired by Trump's description of Clinton, made a similar suggestion on Facebook. The two women decided to combine their events, and the Women's March was born.

Right from the start there was discord. Shook had offered a name for the event:

## KIMBERLÉ CRENSHAW ON INTERSECTIONALITY

Kimberlé Crenshaw is a legal scholar who began thinking about how discrimination that is based on more than one thing has to be made visible in order to fight it. She writes:

> Intersectionality is an analytic sensibility, a way of thinking about identity and its relationship to power. Originally articulated on behalf of black women . . . intersectional erasures are not exclusive to black women. People of color within LGBTQ movements; girls of color in the fight against the school-to-prison pipeline; women within immigration movements; trans women within feminist movements; and people with disabilities fighting police abuse—all face vulnerabilities that reflect the intersections of racism, sexism, class oppression, transphobia, able-ism and more. Intersectionality has given many advocates a way to frame their circumstances and to fight for their visibility and inclusion.[5]

The Million Woman March. Yet there had already been a Million Woman March on October 25, 1997, in Philadelphia, Pennsylvania. Unlike the protest proposed by Bland and Shook, that grassroots gathering had been organized largely by local African-American women. It was a call for unity to support families and solidarity to confront such problems as crime and poverty in the inner cities, inequality in public education, and the war on drugs. Speakers included US Representative Maxine Waters and South African activist Winnie Mandela. It was also a daylong exploration of what it means to be a woman of African-American descent in the United States. An estimated 300,000 to 1.5 million attended the 1997 Million

US Representative Maxine Waters represents California's 43rd district in the House of Representatives.

Woman March, which was held two years after the Million Man March on Washington, an event focusing on African-American men.[6]

The actual name of the march was just the tip of the iceberg. What lay beneath was a demand for awareness and inclusion. On the event's Facebook page, someone wrote: "I will not even consider supporting this until the organizers are intersectional, original and come up with a different name."[7]

## WHAT IS INTERSECTIONALITY?

Intersectionality is a way of analyzing society based on the intersections, or places of overlap, between layers of oppression based on race, class, gender, sexual orientation, disability, and other factors. The term *intersectionality* was coined nearly 30 years ago by African-American civil rights advocate Kimberlé Crenshaw.

## UNPACKING WHITE PRIVILEGE

*White privilege* is a term that is important to intersectionality. What is white privilege, and why is it important to understand it? It describes the advantages, both subtle and obvious, that white people experience because of their race. The critical scholar Peggy McIntosh explains how white privilege is an "invisible" advantage:

> I think whites are carefully taught not to recognize white privilege, as males are taught not to recognize male privilege. I have come to see white privilege as an invisible package of unearned assets that I can count on cashing in each day, but about which I was "meant" to remain oblivious. White privilege is like an invisible weightless knapsack of special provisions, maps, passports, codebooks, visas, clothes, tools, and blank checks. Describing white privilege makes one newly accountable.[8]

Crenshaw argued that the experiences of African-American women could be understood by combining the separate layers of racism and sexism. Intersectionality is a framework that calls for a more nuanced and complex way of understanding how oppression is linked in its many dimensions. White women were now being asked to acknowledge privileges of race and class, as well as the history of racism. Racism had been a factor in feminist movements in the past. For example, the organizers of a 1913 march on Washington, DC, for women's right to vote

Crenshaw's concept of intersectionality has been deeply influential.

asked African-American women to march at the back of the parade.

By calling for an intersectional approach to the proposed Women's March, critics were demanding that

## RESISTING THE "OPPRESSION OLYMPICS"

In *Black Feminist Thought*, published in 1990, Patricia Hill Collins writes about what she calls "standpoint theory." She explains how each group speaks from its own standpoint and shares its partial truth. Admitting one's standpoint and bias is more credible than claiming they are universal. Taking the focus off dominant groups is important, as is admitting that one's own group may not be the most oppressed group in a particular context. The so-called Oppression Olympics is the claim that one's own group suffers the most, and it's a way of competing when it comes to oppression. An intersectional approach resists this notion, which can blind members of one group to the disadvantages of others. Instead of competition, intersectionality encourages cooperation and solidarity.

it encompass a much broader perspective than that of the mostly white women organizing it. The response was to bring a diverse group of organizers into leadership positions. They included Linda Sarsour of the Arab American Association of New York, gun control activist Tamika Mallory, and Carmen Perez, executive director of the nonprofit organization The Gathering for Justice. Responses by white women were mixed, especially after Rose's blog post. She advised white women to wake up to the racism African-American women know all too well. Some white women canceled their plans to participate. "This is a women's march," said one white woman. "We're supposed to be allies in equal pay, marriage, adoption. Why is it now about, 'White women don't understand black women'?"[9]

In the end, the Women's March organizers compiled a three-page unity policy statement that reflected an intersectional approach. It included economic justice, reproductive freedom, immigration reform, police accountability, and union rights. What began in contention evolved into a continuing dialogue on intersectionality. Marchers and supporters considered how race, gender, class, immigration status, sexual orientation, and so many other facets of identity are all vital to understanding social justice. From these conversations arose one of the largest days of protest in history.

# DISCUSSION STARTERS

- Based on what you have read, do you feel the criticisms of the Women's March by women of color were valid? Why or why not? What would you have done differently if you were organizing the march?

- Have you ever experienced or witnessed an example of white privilege? If so, what did you think about it?

- Do you think intersectionality is a helpful tool for understanding racism and sexism? Why or why not? How do you think intersectionality and white privilege are connected?

- Can you give a specific example of how focusing only on the oppression of your own identity group might blind you to the oppression of another group? What could you do to prevent this?

# CHAPTER TWO

# INVISIBLE
# SOLDIERS

SOJOURNER TRUTH.

# NARRATIVE

OF

# SOJOURNER TRUTH,

A

# NORTHERN SLAVE,

EMANCIPATED FROM BODILY SERVITUDE BY THE STATE OF

NEW YORK, IN 1828.

## WITH A PORTRAIT.

---

'Sweet is the virgin honey, though the wild bee store it in a reed;
And bright the jewelled band that circleth an Ethiop's arm;
Pure are the grains of gold in the turbid stream of the Ganges;
And fair the living flowers that spring from the dull cold sod.
Wherefore, thou gentle student, ber d thine ear to my speech,
For I also am as thou art; our hearts can commune together:
To meanest matters will I stoop, for mean is the lot of mortal;
I will rise to noblest themes, for the soul hath a heritage of glory.'

BOSTON:
PRINTED FOR THE AUTHOR.
1850.

If she were alive today, Sojourner Truth might have been
a blogger, in demand as a speaker at college campuses,
with podcasts downloaded by millions. But back in the
days before the Civil War (1861–1865), she had to deliver
her message one speech at a time. Born into slavery as
Isabella Baumfree, she chose her own name, remaking
herself as a fiery speaker for the abolitionist and women's
suffrage movements. She escaped slavery and became the
first black woman to successfully sue a white man for the
return of an enslaved child.

Truth gave her most famous speech in 1851 at the
Women's Rights Convention in Akron, Ohio. Long
before the term *intersectionality* was ever invented, her
speech "Ain't I a Woman?" was a raw testimony to the
intersection of race and gender. She began by mocking
the commonplace assumption that women are so fragile
that they need to be helped into carriages and lifted over
ditches. In saying this, she did not state the obvious: in her
time, only white women of a certain class were treated
this way.

Truth then pointed out the stark contrast between
this view of white women and the harsh way she had
been treated:

*I could work as much and eat as much as a man—when I could get it—and bear the lash as well! And ain't I a woman? I have borne thirteen children, and seen most all sold off to slavery, and when I cried out with my mother's grief, none but Jesus heard me! And ain't I a woman?[1]*

Truth's passionate speeches were precursors to modern concepts of intersectionality.

## "SI, SE PUEDE!"

The Chicano movement of the 1960s and 1970s was partly inspired by the civil rights movement, and it grew to address worker rights, racism, and exploitation as experienced by Mexican Americans. Women played a role in this movement, but it was largely led by men. In response, Chicana women formed the Comisión Femenil Mexicana Nacional (CFMN) in 1970. They focused on the criminal justice system, gendered violence, and women's health. Labor leader and civil rights activist Dolores Huerta was a keynote speaker at a CFMN conference. She popularized the phrase "Si, se puede," later adapted by Barack Obama in its English form, "Yes, we can," during his campaign for president.[2] Her image has appeared in many murals around the country. In 1993, Huerta was the first Latina inducted into the National Women's Hall of Fame. She received the Presidential Medal of Freedom in 2012.

For centuries, women of color such as Truth have struggled at the forefront of social change. Unlike Truth, however, the majority were not given a place of honor in US history. Instead, their names were erased from history. They are the invisible soldiers in social movements such as abolition, women's suffrage, anti-lynching, civil rights, and women's rights. Only now are their vital contributions being more fully acknowledged.

Women of color have always played an important role in US movements for social justice. The poet Phillis Wheatley and the escaped slaves Harriet Jacobs and Harriet Tubman fought against slavery. The activist Mary Church Terrell and journalist Ida B. Wells fought against lynching. Civil rights workers Septima Clark, Fannie Lou Hamer, and Dorothy Height fought against discrimination. Shirley Chisolm, Alice Walker, Angela Davis, and others fought against racism and sexism. They are just a few of the many who have been warriors in the battle for social justice.

## MOVING ROSA'S HOUSE

Even those activists whose names are well known have often not been given the respect their achievements would deserve. One example of this can be seen with Rosa Parks. Her story is familiar to many Americans. In 1955, after refusing to give up her seat at the front of a bus to a white man, she was arrested. Her arrest led to the Montgomery, Alabama, bus boycott against segregation and contributed to the rise of the civil rights movement.

Rosa Parks's home, like the homes of many important people in US history, has been recognized as a historical landmark. Yet for a time it did not stand in its original location in Detroit, Michigan. Instead, it was in Berlin, Germany. When artist Ryan Mendoza learned her home was going to be demolished, he took it apart piece by piece to be shipped to Berlin in April 2017. It stood as both a monument and a rebuke. Mendoza says the Berlin location was symbolic. He draws a connection between Berlin—which was once separated by a wall into East Berlin and West Berlin—and the United States, where

Rosa Parks's reassembled house stood for a time among modern buildings in Berlin, Germany.

President Trump vowed to build a wall on the nation's southern border: "It's resurrected in the month of Easter in a city reborn after a wall was taken down and was not valued in a country that's intent on building a wall."[3] In September 2017, a US foundation pledged to provide funding to bring the house home to the United States, where it would be placed at a university or a museum.

## THE POWER OF WORDS

Names and terms in society can have considerable power and meaning. These names and the way they organize people can prove controversial. One common term for women belonging to racial minorities, *women of color*, is an example of this. Some argue this term blurs distinctions of privilege within

## WOMEN OF ALL RED NATIONS

Some American Indian women activists have not wanted to be associated with feminism, even though they face a high rate of gendered violence. Feminism was not considered useful in creating a united front for the battle against white oppression. Other women of color, particularly from non-Western countries, have expressed the same concerns. Lorelei DeCora Means, one of the founders of Women of All Red Nations, said:

*We are American Indian women, in that order. We are oppressed, first and foremost, as American Indians, as peoples colonized by the United States of America, not as women. As Indians, we can never forget that. Our survival, the survival of every one of us—man, woman and child—as Indians depends on it. Decolonization is the agenda, the whole agenda, and until it is accomplished, it is the only agenda that counts for American Indians. You start to get the idea maybe all this feminism business is just another extension of the same old racist, colonialist mentality.[4]*

## INTERSECTIONALITY AND THIRD-WAVE FEMINISM

The women's movement has often been described in three phases, or "waves." First-wave feminism focused on obtaining rights, such as the right to vote and the right to own and inherit property. Second-wave feminism began in the 1960s and addressed broader issues, such as gendered violence and workplace discrimination. Third-wave feminism is considered intersectional, with a broad focus on patriarchy and other forms of oppression. It is the kind of feminism that was highlighted by organizers of the Women's March on Washington.

the diversity of groups it claims to describe. For example, the writer Jhumpa Lahiri, whose Indian-born parents were professionals in Rhode Island, did not experience the same kind of discrimination as author Sandra Cisneros, a Chicana who grew up in working-class Chicago. Should they be grouped together as women of color?

Activist Loretta Ross explains that the term was born in 1977 at the National Women's Conference in Houston, Texas. It was proposed by black feminists who wanted to express the need for a minority women's platform to speak to a different set of issues than those addressed by largely white middle-class women. It was a way to encompass all minority women and make visible their political and social concerns, both to white women and to men of all races.

There are some shared concerns that can unite women of color, regardless of their individual backgrounds. One of the most important is the complicated set of ways that racism and sexism influence their lives. Equally critical is their relationship to patriarchy, the structures in society that empower men at the expense of women. Other shared concerns for women of color include vulnerability to violence and its effects; disparity in health and pay; stereotypes and bias at school, on the job, and in the media; and lack of leadership opportunities. Just as Sojourner Truth chose her own name as an act of empowerment, women of color have chosen to come together in order to better understand how what divides them can be less powerful than what unites them.

# DISCUSSION STARTERS

- Throughout history, women of color have often been made to give up leadership roles to black men and to white women. What do you think are the reasons for this?

- What does it mean to be an "invisible soldier"? How can these people be made visible?

- Do you think it matters that Rosa Parks's house was for a time in Berlin? Why or why not?

- What do you think of the term women of color? What are some differences among the groups defined in that phrase? What are some shared concerns?

# CHAPTER THREE

# SPEAKING UP, FIGHTING BACK

While the kidnapping, rape, torture, and sexual slavery of girls and women has existed for as long as humans have, this type of abuse is particularly relevant for women of color. Violence is easier when its victims are seen as less than human. Millions of black enslaved women were treated as property, brutalized and raped with impunity by their owners, and forced to produce offspring.

With American Indians, being seen as lesser has also had tragic consequences. Children were removed from families and taken to American Indian boarding schools and foster care. Some were subjected to sexual and physical abuse, and some underwent forced sterilization. As American Indian, lesbian author Judith Witherow explains, "If someone is deemed impure, sexually perverse, dirty, barbaric, rapable, etc. then justification for annihilation is not just a statement—it is permission to rid the land of any trace of the original inhabitants."[1]

## VIOLENCE AND CHINESE WOMEN

There are several kinds of violence to which women of color are particularly vulnerable. The treatment of Americans Indians and enslaved black women is relatively well known. However, less familiar is the treatment of Chinese women, particularly in the western states. From

In the 1800s, Chinese women and girls who came to the United States were subject to discrimination and abuse.

the beginning of their immigration to the United States in the 1800s, which was restricted due to racism, the Chinese faced constant discrimination.

# HUMAN TRAFFICKING

Certain populations are at high risk for human trafficking. Not surprisingly, these include women and girls facing labor exploitation; survivors of domestic violence, sexual assault or child abuse; and runaways and the homeless. Since the majority of human trafficking victims are girls and women, and more than 70 percent of people who are trafficked are people of color, it follows that girls and women of color are especially vulnerable.[2] It is extremely difficult to estimate the true number of girls and women of color who are enduring this form of modern-day slavery. This is because most of them are forced to be silent, threatened with violence, death, and—if they are not US citizens—deportation. In 2012, there were an estimated 20.9 million human trafficking victims worldwide. The United Nations has identified sexual exploitation as the most commonly identified type of trafficking. In the United States, more than 5,000 cases of sex trafficking were reported in 2016.[3]

They were often forced to live in segregated areas known as Chinatowns. Because of restrictive and racist immigration laws, there were fewer women than single men, who were allowed to enter the country as laborers to perform dangerous work in gold mines and on railroads. There were also penalties and laws against interracial marriages and interracial sex.

These factors, along with cultural and linguistic barriers, forced many Chinese women into prostitution. Most Chinese prostitutes were kidnapped or lured with promises of work, or they had been purchased and sold as babies or girls for thousands of dollars. They were kept as prisoners in brothels, enduring physical and mental abuse.

When they came down with sexually transmitted diseases, such as syphilis, they were left untreated. Their average life span as prostitutes was only four years. In 1870 in San Francisco, California, 50 to 75 percent of all adult Chinese women were prostitutes.[4] In addition to this sexual trafficking and slavery, Chinese women were also the victims of broader anti-Chinese mob violence that included forced removals and lynching.

Although these examples illustrate the ways in which the dominant culture works to create violence toward women of color, violence within communities of color also makes women and girls more vulnerable. In the case of Chinese women, many were victims of a practice called foot-binding. This involved breaking the bones of the feet and preventing normal growth by wrapping them tightly, all because a small foot was considered desirable.

The girls endured severe pain growing up, and they were eventually unable to stand and walk on their own without great difficulty. Unfortunately, such violence was perpetuated by other women, mothers of the merchant and landlord classes. Their daughters were not expected to work. This cultural practice was part of Chinese tradition for more than 1,000 years, and it lasted into the early 1900s in Chinese American communities.

## GENDER-BASED VIOLENCE

For black women, gendered violence was a constant fact of life under slavery and its aftermath, during which they faced the relentless reality of rape and sexual violence without any hope of help from the law. Gender-based violence is violence directed against girls and women because of their gender, or violence that affects girls and women disproportionately, such as rape, stalking, domestic violence, and sex trafficking.

In addition to gender-based violence, there are pressures of patriarchal culture that continue to exist in many traditional societies around the world, where the notion of so-called sexual purity is tied to family honor. The female victims, rather than the perpetrators, are

## LATINAS AND DOMESTIC VIOLENCE

According to the National Latin@ Network, one in three Latinas have experienced domestic violence.[5] Studies indicate that Latinas who are abused, as well as youth who witness this abuse, are at a higher risk for poor health. More married immigrant women than unmarried experience domestic violence. A 2009 study also indicates that Latinas who have suffered domestic violence and intimate-partner abuse suffered more than their peers from mental health problems, such as depression, substance abuse, post-traumatic stress disorder, and thoughts of suicide. When adjusting for race and ethnicity, women with a lifetime of intimate-partner violence had significantly more mental health problems than nonabused women, and these problems were more pronounced in Latina women. Reasons for this could include cultural values, such as the central importance of family, gender role expectations, religion, as well as a fear of deportation and a hostile anti-immigration environment.

sometimes shamed. In Nigeria, for example, nearly 300 teenage girls were kidnapped by the extremist group Boko Haram in 2014. The girls who have survived to be released often face ostracism. They are viewed as "spoiled," and they must endure a double burden of trauma: that of a survivor, and that of a bearer of shame.[6]

Such gender-based violence also occurs in the United States. In 2014, the Department of Justice estimated that approximately two dozen so-called honor killings take place in the country each year.[7] Due to inconsistent and inadequate statistics and tracking of murders, exact figures are not available.

# A CULTURE OF SILENCE

Throughout American history, thousands of black men were routinely lynched and brutalized

## MASCULINITY AND GENDERED VIOLENCE

The former National Football League quarterback Donald McPherson has devoted years to raising awareness about all forms of violence against women, and he has taken this message to college campuses across the nation. Campus violence against women is coming under scrutiny, thanks to such documentaries as *The Hunting Ground*, which spotlight sexual assault on campuses. McPherson believes men need to change the way they think and behave toward women. He thinks they are socialized to view their masculinity at the expense of women. For example, saying that a young man does something "like a girl" is seen as a great insult, as is calling him "gay." McPherson urges men to respect others by respecting themselves: "Each generation we have to get better, we need to address the narrowness of what it means to be a man. Words matter and they cut deep."[8]

A racist mob destroyed homes and businesses in Rosewood, Florida.

for unfounded charges of rape against white women. Perhaps the most well-known example is that of the teenager Emmett Till, who allegedly whistled at a white woman—and who was brutally murdered by white men a few days later. His mother chose to leave his casket open as a statement, and a photograph of his battered body was featured in media around the world. Besides the countless instances of such violence inflicted against black men, entire black communities could also be demolished. In 1923, a Florida town called Rosewood was completely destroyed by a white mob based on a white woman's accusation of attack by a black man.

Despite this history, there exists a complex culture of silence around rape. Rape is an underreported crime across all races, but it is least reported among African-American women. One reason is the mistrust of the criminal justice system and the police. Another is that the majority of women are raped by someone they know. When their attacker is also

## DIAMOND REYNOLDS

On July 6, 2016, Diamond Reynolds of Minnesota found herself at the center of national media attention. That evening, she sat in the passenger seat of a car driven by her boyfriend, Philando Castile. Both are African American. Reynolds's four-year-old daughter was in the back seat. A police officer pulled them over in a suburb of Saint Paul, the state capital. After the officer approached the driver's window, Castile informed the officer that he was legally carrying a firearm. The officer reached for his own gun and told Castile not to pull out the gun. Both Castile and Reynolds insisted Castile was not reaching for the gun. The officer then fired seven shots at Castile, killing him. Seconds later, Reynolds began streaming video of the aftermath on Facebook to ensure what had happened would be recorded. The next year, Reynolds testified in court after the officer was put on trial. Explaining her decision to immediately stream video from the car, she said, "I know that the people are not protected against the police."⁹ The officer was later acquitted, leading to widespread protests and outrage.

black or Latino, there is added pressure for those women. They may be made to feel that at all costs they must protect their communities, and—in the case of incest—their families.

Fortunately, change is happening. It is often led by other women of color who are survivors of violence. They are speaking up and breaking the silence, offering special counseling and workshops specifically designed to help women of color. Across the country, they are finding ways to tackle the many challenges violence, both gender based and more general, presents to women of color.

The activist group Black Lives Matter was founded by three women of color, Alicia Garza, Patrisse Cullors, and Opal Tometi. Angie Thomas's young adult novel, *The Hate U Give*, is about a young black woman who turns to activism after losing two of her closest friends to gun violence. In East Los Angeles, the Ovarian Psycos Cycle Brigade is an innovative women's bicycle brigade that uses activism by predominately Latina survivors of trauma and violence to reclaim their community, which was the birthplace of the Chicano Rights movement. In the end, safety from violence is not just a woman's right, but a human right. Women of color can help lead the struggle to find ways of ensuring the right to be safe from violence and the right to justice for its victims and survivors.

# DISCUSSION STARTERS

- What are some reasons that victims and survivors of violence who are women of color may underreport the crimes against them?
- What does gender-based violence mean to you? In what ways are women of color more vulnerable to gendered violence and to human trafficking?
- Do you think that violent movies, music, video games, and sports contribute to violence against women? Why or why not?

# SILENT
# KILLERS

Imagine a preventable disease that kills women of color in the United States two times more often than white women. That rate of death is closer to that of poor countries in Africa and Latin America. The disease is not breast cancer or heart disease. It is cervical cancer. Despite this, there is much less public and media attention to cervical cancer and the shockingly large, deadly gap between white women and women of color.

Recent studies indicate that the death rate for cervical cancer among black women is 10.1 per 100,000. For white women, it is 4.7 per 100,000.[1] But the numbers tell only part of the story. The evidence for why a treatable disease that is fairly rare among white women is deadly for women of color points to inequalities in the health-care system.

There are innovative solutions to a problem such as

## HEALTH GAPS

In 2014 the National Institutes of Health's Office of Research on Women's Health published a comprehensive data book on the health of women of color and the factors affecting their health. The findings are organized to highlight American Indians and Alaska Natives, Native Hawaiians and other Pacific Islanders, Hispanics/Latinos, Blacks/African Americans, and Asian Americans. The report contains important information that can help change the health gap through education, better access, and lifestyle changes for prevention. Significantly, African-American women die at a higher rate from heart disease, cancer, and stroke than any other group.

this one. Mobile clinics, access to vaccines, and one-step tests that don't require follow-up visits and costly procedures could help reduce inequality. Yet measures such as these are underfunded and not the norm. This deadly disparity that affects women of color is reflected in the lack of public response.

## HEALTH DISPARITIES

Health insurance coverage is one important factor. Approximately 37 percent of Hispanic women and one-third of black women lacked health coverage in 2013, compared with just 12 percent of white women.[2] Women of color face profoundly greater barriers when it comes to health-care access, and this is one of the most glaring examples of how the lives of women of color are different from those of white women.

By 2017, the Affordable Care Act (ACA), commonly known as Obamacare, was on its way to decreasing the disparities in health insurance coverage, significantly increasing coverage among women of color. The gap between Asian American and white women had nearly disappeared. However, political turmoil in 2017 left the future of the ACA uncertain.

Volunteers prepared to provide free treatment to uninsured people at a temporary clinic in Washington, DC, in 2010.

# RISKS AND BARRIERS

Women of color dying from cervical cancer represent only one example of health disparities. Their children are also at risk. On average, black infants die at twice the rate of white infants. And in one Washington, DC, neighborhood, the rate is even higher, with black babies dying at ten times the rate of the white babies nearby.[3]

The American health-care system has often failed to provide for women of color. A major problem has been, and continues to be, one of access. In the past, many white doctors would simply refuse to see women of color. Segregated hospitals meant that some patients died before they could see a doctor. Among African Americans, there was also a mistrust of the medical establishment. Doctors had carried out experiments on black patients without

## HENRIETTA LACKS

When she died in 1951, Henrietta Lacks could never have imagined that her cells would go on to be used in worldwide scientific research—and that her story would inspire both a book and a film. During her time as a patient at Johns Hopkins Hospital in Baltimore, Maryland, Lacks's cells were taken without her permission during a biopsy for cervical cancer. Her cells continued growing in a laboratory petri dish. They were the first human cells ever to be reproduced this way. Scientists used her cells in 60,000 scientific studies.[4] They made major breakthroughs in medical research, improving the understanding of cancer and aging. But Lacks's family was not told about this until 1973, and they were not compensated for the use of her cells. Her story inspired the 2010 book *The Immortal Life of Henrietta Lacks* and its 2017 film adaptation.

their consent. In the Tuskegee syphilis experiments, which occurred between the 1930s and the 1970s, researchers purposefully did not treat some black patients suffering from syphilis, instead observing the patients to see how the disease progressed.

Barriers to health care have been slow to vanish for women of color. When inexpensive local clinics, such as Planned Parenthood locations, are closed, it is poor women of color who bear the greatest burden, losing access to basic women's health care, including Pap tests and other exams that screen for preventable diseases. When government aid programs such as the Special Supplemental Nutrition Program for Women, Infants, and Children (WIC) have their budgets slashed, it is again poor women of color who will feel the greatest impact. When fresh, healthful foods are unavailable to residents of inner-city areas, creating what are known as food deserts, eating a balanced diet to prevent obesity, diabetes, and heart disease becomes much more difficult. Exercise, too, is much more difficult to get when there are no safe spaces to exercise in the inner city and when people have no spare time after working multiple jobs. All of these factors affect health and mortality rates.

## THE THREAT OF CHRONIC STRESS

Heart disease, diabetes, breast cancer, stroke: across the board, women of color die from these conditions more often than any other group. When it comes to the diseases that are the result of chronic stress, women of color fare even worse.

Stress is not always a bad thing. The body and mind perceive what they consider threats, both large and small. The body uses its stress response mechanism, releasing a group of hormones when it's faced with a situation in which it must fight, flee, or freeze. In prehistoric times, this response was critical to survival. Adrenaline pumped through the body, the heart rate went up, and the legs began moving to fight or flee the danger coming. In some cases, the body went limp to freeze and hide from danger. Modern dangers and challenges still trigger the stress response. The problem with this response is when it doesn't stop, it turns into something more harmful.

Chronic stress can lead to hypertension, heart disease, diabetes, stroke, and other conditions that kill women of color at a higher rate than any other group of people in the United States. Chronic stress is often linked to traumatic experiences, such as violence in the home and neighborhood, childhood physical and sexual abuse,

HIV/AIDS and women of color

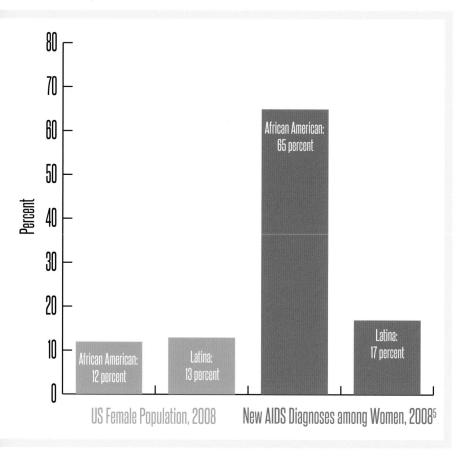

poverty, and other stressors. It is worsened by ways that racism and sexism affect women of color.

Many women of color develop chronic stress because they feel they must support their entire families, holding down jobs while caring for children and aging relatives. In trying their best to care for everyone around them, they often neglect to care for themselves. Mental health problems are often left untreated because of lingering stigma for seeking treatment.

## DEATH BY A THOUSAND CUTS

The concept of microaggressions is a useful tool for an intersectional understanding of chronic stress and its impact on women of color. Instead of the dramatic knife wounds of overt racism and sexism, microaggressions are like death by a thousand paper cuts—just as painful, but hard to see one at a time. Microaggressions are the everyday instances of racism faced by people of color. They may be minor when considered alone, and they may even be unintentional. But when added together, their impact can be significant.

For example, in education, an overt form of racism would be to segregate schools or automatically send children of color into remedial classes. Microaggression is subtler. A teacher sees a Latina girl and a white boy

## MEASURING GENDERED RACIAL MICROAGGRESSIONS

Using a framework of intersectionality, researchers have come up with a system to measure the subtle ways that behavior, language, and environment can interact to create gendered racial microaggressions experienced by black women. Four contributing factors stand out. The first is how black women can be objectified, based on their perceived "sexual availability" or their beauty. Second is the experience of being "silenced and marginalized." The third factor is being stereotyped as "strong." Displays of strength that are praised in a man are often criticized as "aggressive" in a woman. The final factor is the stereotype of black women as "angry."[6] The black women who participated in this study reported experiencing stress and psychological distress related to these four factors and the connected microaggressions. Different racial and ethnic groups confront different stereotypes, but silence and marginalization are very common forms of gendered racial microaggression.

who seem to be sitting a little too close to each other during a math test. She immediately assumes the Latina was cheating, although it was actually the white student who was copying her answers. After she hears the full story, the teacher apologizes, but the harm has been done. The teacher may not have jumped to her conclusion with the specific intention of doing harm. She may have simply felt a bias or subtle negative feeling about the intellectual skills of Latina girls. However, the teacher's behavior because of her bias resulted in microaggression.

Microaggressions that specifically affect women of color are also known as gendered racial microaggression. How a young woman of color processes the sum of microaggressions over the course of her life can easily result in chronic stress—and the deadly diseases related to it.

The woman of color's stress response may always be in high gear because the battle against racism and sexism is ongoing. Instead of dealing with stress by overworking, overeating, abusing substances, or numbing out in other ways, women of color can cope through journaling, tuning into emotions and the body through mindfulness, finding supportive peers and mentors, and other forms of self-care. Chronic stress and its diseases may appear invisible, but the body is always keeping score.

# DISCUSSION STARTERS

- Have you ever witnessed or experienced an example of a gendered racial microaggression? If so, what was your reaction?
- Why do you think women of color are more likely to die from treatable diseases, and how can this be changed?
- What do you think health equity means, and how can it be achieved?

# THE
# LONGEST WALK

On a September morning in 1957, two 15-year-olds prepared for school in Little Rock, Arkansas. One chose a white cotton skirt with a petticoat, sewn by her and her sister just for that day. The other picked a sleek light-green dress with a ribbon at the waist, bought from a downtown department store. Neither knew the other existed, but by the end of that tumultuous day, their fates would be tied together.

On September 4, 1957, Elizabeth Eckford, wearing white, was one of nine black students to attempt to integrate Central High School. Hazel Bryan, wearing green, was one member of the white mob that screamed and spat at her. Iconic photos captured Eckford's calm walk and Bryan's anger. Eckford and the other students were blocked from entering the school. The walk to and from school that day felt like the longest of Eckford's life. On September 24, President Dwight Eisenhower sent US Army troops to assist

Federal troops escorted the black students into school.

the students. On September 25, they attended their first full day of school.

The nightmare of the Little Rock Nine, as they came to be called, would continue throughout the school year. They were bullied, beaten, and banned from participating in extracurricular activities. Yet they could not fight back against their tormentors, because they knew that if they did, they would be the ones punished. Following the 1954 Supreme Court decision *Brown v. Board of Education*, in which racial segregation in public schools had been declared illegal, they knew the eyes of the world were on them. Eckford never forgot that year and suffered from the trauma long afterward.

## EDUCATION AND EQUITY

The struggle for education by women like Elizabeth Eckford has been uphill and hard fought. Women of color were at the forefront of the civil rights movement, though more often as invisible soldiers who confronted the constraints of gender, race, and class.

Access to quality education is still an ongoing challenge for girls and women of color. It is especially so for those who are poor and rely on public education and government programs. Education is critically important. Former President Barack Obama stated, "We are true to our creed when a little girl born into the bleakest poverty knows that she has the same chance to succeed as anybody else."[1]

One of the best indicators of children's success in school and their overall health is their mother's level of education. Breaking the cycle of poverty, the tendency of children of impoverished parents to remain in poverty themselves, is nearly impossible without ensuring the education of girls. This is true not only in the United States but around the world.

Keeping these facts in mind, it's important to remember that equity and equality are not the same thing. Equity is giving everyone a chance to be successful. Equality is treating everyone in the same way. For a girl of color growing up in poverty, what she needs to be successful will be different than what a white middle-class

## WHAT DOES "ACTING WHITE" MEAN?

The "acting white" theory first emerged from 1980s research claiming that black students who did well in school were often accused of being disloyal to their race, or "acting white." This research became so well known that in 2004, then-Senator Obama referred to it in a speech: "Children can't achieve unless we raise their expectations and turn off the television sets and eradicate the slander that says a black youth with a book is acting white."[2] However, further research has cast some doubt on the original conclusions. A national survey of high school students found that 95 percent of black girls were proud of doing well in school and were also higher achievers when their mothers had college degrees.[3]

## EDUCATION AND A FEAR OF DEPORTATION

In December 2016, Senator Rick Santorum was taking part in a town hall event when Elizabeth Vilchis exchanged words with him. Vilchis spoke about her experience leaving Mexico as a young girl and becoming a mechanical engineer. She has been undocumented ever since, but she has used her skills to inspire young people in her community to pursue science, technology, engineering, and math careers. She worried about the incoming Trump administration's policies about immigration: "I will lose my career and I will also potentially be labeled for deportation, which means I will be removed from the communities I have contributed to so much. As 2017 starts, I'd like to ask for your advice on how to plan for my future and what lays ahead."[5] Santorum suggested that Vilchis go to another country, "be successful and reapply to come back to America."[6]

boy will need. Equality doesn't factor in that difference. Equity does.

For girls and women of color facing gendered racism and microaggressions, education can be a path to opportunity, though there are still obstacles ahead of them. On the one hand, women of color have surpassed their male counterparts when it comes to earning college degrees, with graduation rates of Hispanic women growing the most.

Yet these advancements still fall short of the degrees earned by white women and white men. The American economy is shifting from manufacturing and service to the technology sector. By 2020, 65 percent of jobs will require a postsecondary degree.[4] Women of color, particularly African Americans, Hispanics, and American Indians, still face significant obstacles, both financially and academically, in earning college degrees. They are also severely underrepresented in the fields of science, engineering, and information technology, where more lucrative jobs are available.

## THE "MODEL MINORITY"

By contrast, Asian women actually have the highest college graduation rate of all women. In 2010, Asian women, despite making up only 5 percent of the population, managed to earn 8 percent of bachelor's degrees.[7] For this and other reasons, some people have stereotypically described Asians as a "model minority."

To be a model minority means there are expectations about certain kinds of behavior,

## AMERICAN INDIAN WOMEN AND EDUCATION

Formal education has and continues to be a source of empowerment for American Indian women. However, federal funding for American Indian education has declined, and the majority of American Indian students are in public schools. They experience high dropout rates, low achievement, and poor self-esteem. American Indian women continue to assume the traditional leadership roles in their cultures. Despite the earlier US policy of forced removal to boarding schools, American Indian women have kept their responsibilities as the keepers of their culture.

such as being good in math and science. But in reality, being a model minority is just as much a stereotype as the negative stereotypes about black and Hispanic women. No minority group is all the same. In the case of Southeast Asians of Cambodian, Hmong, and Laotian heritage, a

The "model minority" phenomenon can put additional pressure on Asian American students.

study found that they actually earn college degrees at a lower rate than the national average. The model minority stereotype can hide real problems such as poverty and isolation and prevent them from being addressed.

Any stereotype, even a seemingly positive one, can make people feel trapped and not allowed to be themselves. For Asian American women aged 15 to 24, suicide is the second-leading cause of death. This is the highest suicide rate of women of any race and ethnicity in that age group.

One reason is that the pressure to succeed can become overwhelming. Professor Eliza Noh, whose sister committed suicide in college, has studied this problem and believes the issue is complex. Generally, in Asian cultures, obedience to one's parents is expected, and parents are stricter with girls than boys. Girls are especially not allowed to express anger or rebellion, and this can turn inward, becoming depression. In fact, a recent collection of essays by American women from South Asia is titled *Good Girls Marry Doctors: South Asian American Daughters on Obedience and Rebellion*. The writers discuss their lack of representation in the media, their feelings of being outsiders in school, and the pressure of parental expectations.

"In my study, the model minority pressure is a huge factor," says Noh, who studied 41 Asian American women who'd attempted or contemplated suicide. "Sometimes it's very overt—parents say, 'You must choose this major or this type of job' or 'You should not bring home As and Bs, only As,'" she says. "And girls have to be the perfect mother and daughter and wife as well."[8]

## EDUCATION AND MARRIAGE

For other women of color, succeeding in the classroom can lead to other pressures as well. The concept of assortative mating describes the desire to find a partner with the same educational level and socioeconomic status. With more women of color surpassing their male counterparts in earning college degrees, the pool of available partners becomes increasingly small, especially when college-educated men of color choose to date or marry people of other ethnicities. Black women have the greatest problems in this regard. They have the lowest rate of marrying across racial lines, partly because of racist attitudes in society to the interracial marriages of black women with men of other races. Less than half of college-educated black women marry a man with some postsecondary education, compared to 84 percent of white college-educated women.[9]

Despite these and other challenges, women of color are making progress in education, and they continue to break down barriers to educational equity. Many have struggled and suffered for the right to learn and to reach their fullest potential, and their long walk continues today.

# DISCUSSION STARTERS

- Have you ever been accused of "acting white" or witnessed someone in that situation? If so, how did you or the person respond?

- In what ways are equality and equity different? What's a specific example you can think of from your own life?

- What are the pros and cons of being considered a model minority? Have you witnessed or experienced this in your school or community, and if you have, how did you feel about it?

- What do you think are the reasons that Hazel Bryan and others acted against the Little Rock Nine the way they did? Are there similar situations you have seen or experienced?

# CHAPTER SIX

# WOMEN OF COLOR
# IN THE
# WORKFORCE

Long before there were well-defined jobs or careers, human beings had to hunt, grow and harvest crops, find drinkable water, and perform the countless acts that helped them survive. For the vast majority of the world's people, work remains a means to an end. The goal is to take care of survival and safety. However, in the United States and other industrialized nations, many people believe work should do more than provide a paycheck. Even so, many working women of color find themselves living from paycheck to paycheck.

Women of color are more than twice as likely to be poor as white men.[1] The gender wage gap, overrepresentation in low-wage jobs because of discrimination and family responsibilities, and higher unemployment are among the reasons for this. Women of color can suffer the damaging compound effects of economic insecurity throughout their lives and transfer this deficit to future generations.

# THE GENDER WAGE GAP

Despite centuries of struggle, there continues to be a significant wage gap between women and men. On average, women earn only 77 cents for every dollar a man makes. Gaps exist between for women of color, too. For

African American women, it's 64 cents for every dollar a white woman makes, and Hispanic women 55 cents. These women also earn less than their male counterparts of the same racial or ethnic group.[2] These numbers tell a sobering story of economic insecurity.

Closing the wage gap would result in women earning approximately $10,000 more a year.[3] That would add up to hundreds of thousands of dollars during the working life of a woman. Despite this economic injustice, the reasons for the wage gap have not disappeared. Women are still paid less than men for the same work, in nearly all occupations and with all levels of education.

Women of color are still overrepresented in low-wage jobs and underrepresented in

## THE HIGH COST OF INCARCERATION

More than half of black women have been incarcerated or have family members or close friends who have been incarcerated, compared to 39 percent for Hispanics and 36 percent for whites. They often pay for prison-related costs and debt. "Women of color are carrying the burden," says Gale Muhammad, head of a prison advocacy group. The economic cost of loving someone in prison "has broken the black family," she adds. "You've got women working two or three jobs to keep it together."[4]

There is also a steep increase in the rate of incarceration for women of color. African-American women are three times more likely than white women to be incarcerated, while Hispanic women are 69 percent more likely.[5] They are often the survivors of abuse and the primary caregivers for their families. After their release, they face restricted access to government support. In some states, they cannot work in childcare, nursing, or home health care, fields in which women of color are concentrated.

## AGE DISCRIMINATION AND POVERTY

As the nation's workforce ages, discrimination against women over 50 is a sometimes-invisible but growing problem with serious economic and social consequences. Research indicates that women are clearly penalized more in the workplace for their age than are men, receiving fewer job interviews and offers even with comparable resumes.

Women of color are no exception to this. They face this discrimination earlier and more often than men. This can leave them forced to retire early and with little savings, often because of low-wage jobs with few benefits, and this can lead to extreme poverty in old age, at a critical time when they may be needed to help care for grandchildren and others in the younger generation. Older women of color are particularly at risk, with 1 in 4 American Indian women over the age of 65 living in poverty.[8]

high-wage jobs. Caregivers are still discriminated against and face barriers that result in lower pay. Women's work is even devalued because women do it. A study of more than 50 years of data revealed that when many women moved into a field, wages declined, even taking into account experience, skills, education, race, and region.[6]

## THE LOW-WAGE WORKFORCE

The low-wage workforce is defined as including those workers who earn $10.10 an hour or less. African-American women make up a larger percentage of the low-wage workforce (11.6 percent) than of the overall workforce (6.1 percent). Hispanic women make up 15.0 percent of the low-wage workforce. Asian, Hawaiian, and/or Pacific Islander women make up 4.4 percent of the low-wage workforce.[7]

Women of color often remain stuck in the low-wage sector, in service jobs and the food industry, with few benefits such as paid sick leave or retirement. The United States does not offer national health care or subsidized childcare, and the ACA, which helped women of color get access to health insurance, is likely to be under attack for the foreseeable future.

Women of color make up more than one-third of women who are among the working poor. The share of Latina women working at or below the minimum wage tripled during the Great Recession from 2007 to 2010, while it doubled for African-American and Asian women. Unemployment for women of color followed the same trend, and the unemployment gap with white women has actually increased since 2007.[9] Undocumented women of color often face even greater barriers of language, culture, and education, and they

## POVERTY BY THE NUMBERS

Each year, the US Census Bureau updates the federal poverty threshold, a number based on income and family size. Using US Census data, the National Women's Law Center analyzed poverty rates for women of color. In 2015:

- 23.1 percent of African American women lived in poverty

- 22.7 percent of American Indian women lived in poverty

- 20.9 percent of Hispanic women lived in poverty

- 11.7 percent of Asian women lived in poverty[10]

Women of color with disabilities, those who are the primary breadwinners for their families, and those who are LGBTQ also face a greater risk of living in poverty.

Many citizens have demanded an increase in the minimum wage.

are among the most vulnerable to exploitation.

# ECONOMIC JUSTICE

Women of color are even more vulnerable to exploitation in low-paid, high-stress—and in the case of many undocumented workers—high-danger jobs where they face sexual violence on a daily basis. A strong connection can be made between the overrepresentation of women of color in the low-wage sector and symptoms such as poor health, chronic stress, and depression. This creates a vicious cycle. Being paid less and often being responsible for the household, they accumulate little or no wealth.

Living paycheck to paycheck, with little chance to break the cycle of poverty,

## TAKING ADVANTAGE

Case Farms produces chicken meat. Its poultry processing plants, with sharp blades of all kinds and floors slick with blood from the slaughter of birds, can be dangerous workplaces. Case Farms recruited refugees knowing they were using fake identification. It then used this knowledge to keep them from organizing for better workplace safety, threatening them with deportation. Evodia González Dimas, originally from Mexico, worked at a Case Farms plant. After she was injured on the job in 2006, she spoke to a local newspaper, saying that workers were routinely told to ignore doctors' notes about work restrictions. González was fired. She challenged her firing before the National Labor Relations Board (NLRB). The NLRB ruled in her favor. But it was a hollow victory. The *New Yorker* magazine noted that in 2002, the Supreme Court ruled that "undocumented workers had the right to complain about labor violations, but that companies had no obligation to rehire them or to pay back wages."[11]

Many women of color work in low-wage fields, such as hotel housekeeping.

women of color face greater economic insecurity. In addition, African-American and Latina women face significantly higher poverty and incarceration rates than their white counterparts, and those who are incarcerated face diminished chances for well-paid employment when they are released.

In the world of work, women of color continue to confront multiple forms of discrimination and oppression that must be addressed before progress is made. Policies that would help create equity include increasing the minimum wage, providing caregiver support such as safe and affordable childcare, protecting accessible reproductive rights and women's health care, offering benefits such as paid sick leave and family leave, strengthening laws against discrimination, and most important, closing the wage gap. Economic justice may remain an elusive goal, but for women of color, the effort is vital, now and for generations to come.

# DISCUSSION STARTERS

- Why do you think the gender wage gap continues, and what do you think should be done to close it?

- Do you think undocumented workers should be protected from exploitation? Why or why not?

- What do you think about your state requiring a living wage, which is above minimum wage and enough to live on or above the poverty line? In what ways would it affect the working poor among women of color?

# CHAPTER SEVEN

# LEANING IN,
## DIGGING DEEP

On paper, Sonia Sotomayor's career was outstanding. She earned a full scholarship to Princeton University, and she was the winner of the top prize for undergraduates for both her academic excellence and extracurricular activities. Even more impressive was how she got to Princeton, not as a graduate of an elite private school, but as the valedictorian of an inner-city Catholic high school.

Sotomayor did not grow up privileged. Both of her parents were Spanish-speaking immigrants from Puerto Rico. Her father was an alcoholic, and her hardworking mother was distant, though she bought her daughter the *Encyclopedia Britannica*. This was unusual for the housing projects of the Bronx in New York City. This daughter of immigrants was diagnosed with juvenile diabetes at the age of seven and learned to give herself her daily insulin injections. She spent time with her grandmother, enjoyed reading Nancy Drew mysteries, and watched the television courtroom drama *Perry Mason*. She dreamed of becoming a lawyer. Sotomayor went on to attend Yale Law School, where she was an editor for the *Yale Review*.

So when she was told during a recruitment dinner for a prestigious law firm that she was at Yale only because of affirmative action, a set of policies that favor people in groups that have historically suffered from discrimination, she decided to fight back. She refused to interview with that firm and filed an official complaint with the campus tribunal. It ruled in her favor and sparked a debate that led to an apology published in the *Washington Post*. Sotomayor was already preparing herself for the kind of battle she would face during her confirmation hearings as the first woman of color ever to be nominated to the US Supreme Court.

## THE LEADERSHIP AMBITION GAP

In her book *Lean In: Women, Work, and the Will to Lead*, Facebook chief operating officer Sheryl Sandberg accuses women of having a "leadership ambition gap," of not taking the opportunities for leadership handed to them, of not "leaning in."[1] Yet women of color such as Sotomayor have been "leaning in" for centuries, and they have never lacked the will to lead. Even so, their experience has

## AMBIVALENT PREJUDICE

Psychologist Susan Fiske studies the effects of status, envy, and scorn in management settings. Her theory of ambivalent prejudice explains how emotions influence actions. Bias works in a subtle way. Sexism, racism, anti-immigrant bias, and xenophobia can influence the decisions of "in-group" managers, who may feel more comfortable with others who are like them. This constant bias creates more barriers to advancement for those who are considered part of the "out-group." Women of color who challenge the "high-warmth/ low-competence" stereotypes are often penalized for characteristics, such as assertiveness, that would be rewarded in members of the "in-group," who are usually middle-class white heterosexual males.[2]

been markedly different from that of white women from more-privileged backgrounds.

Once again, it seems the word *women* in Sandberg's title implicitly refers to white women of a privileged socioeconomic status. For these women, opting out of a career to stay at home and care for children is a real possibility. Historically this hasn't been the case for women of color. The feminist author bell hooks describes Sandberg's acceptance of the status quo and refusal to acknowledge her own class privilege as "faux feminism."[3]

# THE TRIPLE GLASS CEILING

Intersectional feminists advocate for changes in society that make it more inclusive and cooperative rather than competitive. Affordable and

Women of color have been underrepresented in government, though many who have reached these positions, such as former Attorney General Loretta Lynch, have been consequential figures.

## A HARD GLASS CEILING

With only a few exceptions, the world of corporate leadership remains closed to women of color. In 2003, media mogul Oprah Winfrey made the *Forbes* magazine billionaire list. She was the first African-American woman to make the list. In the years since, little progress has been made at the top of big business. In 2017, there were no black women leading the top 500 most profitable corporations as ranked by *Fortune* magazine. Even though the 2017 list includes the greatest number of female chief executive officers (CEOs), only two of them are women of color.[5] Geisha Williams, the CEO of the Pacific Gas and Electric Company since March 2017, is the first Latina ever featured on the *Fortune* 500 list. She was born in Cuba and immigrated as a girl to the United States with her family. Indra Nooyi was born in India and moved to the United States to attend the Yale School of Management. The president and CEO of Pepsi, she is frequently named among the world's most powerful women by magazines such as *Forbes* and *Fortune*.

accessible health care and childcare, antidiscrimination laws for women over 50, and related policies could help bring about more justice and equity for women of all classes, races, and sexual orientations.

Many women of color in the United States are all too familiar with being both the primary earners and caretakers in their families. Most have never had the choice to choose one role over the other. Despite their hard work and ambition, they keep bumping up against a triple glass ceiling made up of racism, sexism, and the intersection of the two. Examining why this is so can also help explain why, even with more women of color graduating and working in the professional pipeline, they are nearly invisible in top power positions.

A 2016 study reveals that ambitious women of color, leaning in just as Sandberg advises, are repeatedly sidelined for leadership positions. They are labeled as pushy or bossy, and they have less support and fewer mentors, both of which are essential to success in corporate America. Although they have high representation in the workforce, women of color are the most underrepresented group in the corporate pipeline. The situation is as bad in politics, where women of color are greatly underrepresented in positions of power at all levels of government.

## CAN A WOMAN OF COLOR BE IMPARTIAL?

One reason for this could be the implicit bias that operates in gendered racism. Justice Sotomayor has experienced it throughout her life. She was nominated to the Supreme Court by the nation's first black president, and she was repeatedly asked about a comment she made in a speech about the enlarged perspective that a "wise Latina" would bring to her rulings.[6]

Former Alabama senator Jeff Sessions became the US attorney general in 2017. At the time of Sotomayor's nomination hearings in the summer of 2009, he seemed offended that a woman of color would claim that her own life experience and heritage could enhance her work.

More importantly, he chose to attack her "impartiality," as if to say that white male judges represent a "universal" default mode with less bias than women of color.[7]

In reality, white male privilege can color the perspective of white men even more, especially if they have never acknowledged their own bias. Sessions ended up voting against Sotomayor's confirmation. As a Latina who fought back against discrimination and microaggressions, and who now sits on the nation's highest court, Justice Sotomayor has become a role model for girls and women of color.

In 2015, Loretta Lynch was appointed by former President Obama as the first African-American woman to serve as US attorney general. Like Justice Sotomayor, she was

## POWER PLAYERS

The past few decades have seen some major breakthroughs for women of color in politics. In 1992, Carol Moseley Braun achieved two firsts. She became the first African-American woman elected to the Senate and the first black senator from the Democratic Party. The first two women of color to serve as governors are both Republicans. Susana Martinez is the governor of New Mexico. Nikki Haley was born Nimrata Randhawa, the daughter of immigrants from India. She was governor of South Carolina before being appointed by President Donald Trump as ambassador to the United Nations. She became the first woman of South Asian ancestry to hold both positions. The first woman of color to serve as secretary of state was Condoleezza Rice, appointed by President George W. Bush. In 1989, Rice was also the first African-American director of Soviet and East European affairs on the National Security Council under President George H. W. Bush.

repeatedly pressed by white male senators about her ability to be an "impartial" advocate of the law. In addition, her confirmation hearing was delayed for months, which led Senator Dick Durbin to make a comparison with Rosa Parks, remarking that Lynch was being asked to "sit in the back of the bus when it comes to the Senate calendar."[8]

## BIAS, STEREOTYPES, AND DISCRIMINATION

The constant struggles of women of color such as Sotomayor, and so many others in corporations, politics, and other areas traditionally dominated by white men, can be examined by focusing on the role of bias in decision-making. Bias is a personal inclination to draw conclusions based on prejudice and stereotypes.

For women of color, both bias and stereotypes reinforce the discrimination that keeps them sidelined from leadership positions. One study examined the bias that occurs when white managers believe that women of color are "warm but incompetent," versus the bias against those who are "smart but cold."[9] The first group is perceived as more cooperative and the second as more competitive. With gendered racism, it is much more difficult to overcome such biases that can stereotype women of color in one of two negative categories. The bias can be subtle and go unexamined.

Oprah Winfrey is one of today's best-known black entertainers and business leaders.

## OVERLOOKED AND SIDELINED

Women of color are severely underrepresented in corporate America. According to a 2016 survey, women of color make up just 3 percent of executives (compared to white women at 17 percent) in top positions at 132 companies surveyed. More than two-thirds of *Fortune* 500 companies have no women of color on their boards.[10] Yet, women of color make up 20 percent of the US population.[11] Only 29 percent of black women who responded to the survey reported the best opportunities at their company go to the most deserving employees, compared to 47 percent of white women, 43 percent of Asian women and 41 percent of Hispanic women.[12]

Many women of color are turning to entrepreneurship, where they are making some inroads by opening their own businesses. Businesses owned by black women are the fastest-growing group of women-owned firms. And in 2013, one of every ten women-owned businesses was owned by Latinas.[13] But entrepreneurship, while enticing to many Americans, is a high-risk proposition for those without financial safety nets, and failure often comes at a high cost.

Senator Kamala Harris quickly gained a reputation as a tough questioner at Senate hearings.

## "WE WILL NOT RETREAT"

Although some nations, such as Liberia and India, have had women of color as presidents and prime ministers, women made up just 22.8 percent of the world's parliaments in June 2016.[14] In January 2015, they constituted approximately 17 percent of the world's cabinet positions.[15] In the US Congress, women of color continue to face obstacles at every level. The kind of media coverage given to congresswomen of color negatively affects voter support, which may in turn cause fewer women of color to run for office and to receive the financial support they need when they do run for office.

Even though women of color are still severely underrepresented in Congress as lawmakers, the ones who serve are making their presence felt. Kamala Harris was elected to the Senate in 2016 as a Democrat from California. She is the daughter of a Tamil Indian mother and a Jamaican-American father, and she is

Harris and other politicians appeared at the Women's March to lend their support to the cause.

the first person of South Asian ancestry to serve in the US Senate.

During a Senate hearing, she was constantly interrupted and shushed by her white male colleagues when she tried to question Attorney General Sessions, but Senator Harris refused to be silenced and marginalized by these expressions of microaggression. At the Women's March on Washington, Senator Harris reminded marchers that all issues are women's issues: "We will not retreat when being attacked. We will stand up and we will fight . . . fight for equality, fight for fairness, fight for justice."[16] Women of color in positions of leadership can help lead this struggle as they continue to fight for a place at the table.

# DISCUSSION STARTERS

- Does having women of color in power mean that organizations will become more responsive to their needs? Why or why not?
- What does "leaning in" mean to you? Who are examples of women of color "leaning in"?
- Do you think a woman of color could ever become the US president? If so, describe what characteristics you think she would need to be elected and to succeed.

# I DREAM
# A WORLD

How many young women can say their words have been sampled by Beyoncé, bought for a film by the Academy Award–winning actress Lupita Nyong'o, and honored with a prestigious National Book Critics Circle Award? Chimamanda Ngozi Adichie has experienced all of these accolades. In 2015, *Time* magazine paid tribute to her as one of the 100 most influential people in the world.

The novelist and critic is in excellent company on the *Time* 100 list. Honored with her are other exemplary women of color. They include pioneering ballerina Misty Copeland, educator Kira Orange Jones, and the president of the group Doctors Without Borders, Joanne Liu. The list of high achievers also includes financial titan Mellody Hobson, blogger and feminist critic Anita Sarkeesian, transgender icon Laverne Cox, and Tony Award–winner Audra McDonald. Beyond the United States, the list honors Afghanistan's first lady, Rula Ghani, Guatemalan human rights leader Aura Farfán, Japanese organizing expert Marie Kondo, Nigerian activist Obiageli Ezekwesili, and Pakistani Nobel Peace Prize–winner Malala Yousafzai.

Adichie is at ease crossing the borders of literary fiction, pop culture, academia, and international film. She is just as comfortable with her Nigerian American identity.

She lives for part of the year in her native land of Nigeria and part of the year in the United States, where she attended college, where her husband works, and where her own daughter was born. Immigrant women of color like her show that being a "hyphenated American" does not mean being torn by divided cultural loyalties. Instead, it can be an important opportunity to build bridges across cultures and reclaim feminism as a movement for social justice around the world.

Adichie represents a new kind of feminism that is both intersectional and transnational, which means going beyond national boundaries. In a talk on feminism, she

Adichie, *right*, and other women appeared at the Girls Write Now Awards, run by an organization that mentors and encourages female authors.

## OBJECTIFICATION AND BODY IMAGE

Body image is important to women of color, especially black women, whose bodies have been abused for centuries. Sarah Baartman was a black South African known as "The Hottentot Venus" when she was displayed in sideshows in the early 1800s. Crowds paid to stare at her large buttocks, and so-called scientists considered her the missing link between apes and humans. Her devastating story served as a basis for Suzan-Lori Parks's play "Venus." Not surprisingly, poor body image can lead to mental health problems, such as eating disorders and depression. Even athletes, whose fitness is not in question, are not immune to objectification. The world's highest-paid female athlete and most decorated tennis champion, Serena Williams, has been constantly attacked as "masculine" for her muscular physique. She has been called a "gorilla," "manly," and "savage."[2] Black ballerinas such as Misty Copeland and Michaela DePrince have both discussed the bias they have faced and how they have turned this around by celebrating their differences.

remembered that feminism was a label she resisted as a teenager, especially because the term was first used by a young male friend she was arguing with, and it was not said as a compliment. She was later told by fellow Nigerians and other Africans, both male and female, that feminists were simply women who were unhappy that they couldn't find husbands or women who had read too many Western books. They were angry women who hated men, bras, and African culture.

Resisting all of these pressures, Adichie decided to call herself a "happy African feminist" who wears lip gloss and high heels, not for men but because she feels like being girly.[1] She has written a book on how to raise a feminist daughter, and among her suggestions is rejecting the need to be liked, which she knows all too well from the criticism of her feminism, especially in Nigeria. She feels it is more important to teach girls to be their full selves. Adichie is just one example of a woman of color working to redefine what it means to be masculine and feminine. She wants to reshape society's gender roles to help create a more just society. This is one goal of intersectional feminism.

## UNDERSTANDING WOMEN'S EXPERIENCES

No individual woman represents all experiences for women of color. The term *women of color* is a tool for understanding a variety of shared experiences. There will always be a diversity of experiences based on class, country of origin, culture, ethnicity, sexual orientation and preference, and many other factors.

A meaningful understanding of the challenges facing women of color in the United States includes a transnational perspective. The fastest-growing segment of women of color is Hispanic women, whose family roots may reach to Mexico and other Latin American and South American countries. The trafficking and sexual slavery of girls and women do not respect national borders. Neither do terrorist networks, the drug trade, organized crime, and climate change.

# FROM ANNA MAY WONG TO SHONDALAND

Despite a long history of misrepresentation of women of color, progress is being made, especially in television. In 1951, Anna May Wong made history with her TV show *The Gallery of Madame Liu-Tsong*. This was the first-ever American television show with an Asian American starring in a lead role. However, her career in film and television was limited by stereotypes of Asian women as exotic. Also, since there were still laws in many states against interracial contact and marriage, sponsors were afraid to offend audiences, so women of color could not play romantic leads opposite white men.

Anna May Wong was a pioneering actress who helped open doors for people of color.

It was not until 1968 that *Julia*, starring Diahann Carroll as a nurse, became the first television show to feature a black woman in a nonstereotypical role. But it was also criticized for not taking a political stance at the height of the civil rights movement.

Since the 1960s, women of color have gone on to successful careers on television, in both drama and comedy. Comedians such as Whoopi Goldberg, Wanda Sykes, Margaret Cho, Mindy Kaling of *The Mindy Project*, and Leslie Jones of *Saturday Night Live* have all had successful careers on network and cable. Issa Rae went from YouTube to HBO with her comedy *Insecure*.

Just as important are the powerful women of color creating new images behind the camera. Writer and executive producer Shonda Rhimes runs her own company, Shondaland. It is responsible for her back-to-back television hits, *How to Get Away With Murder* and *Scandal*. In both shows, women of color are the powerful central protagonists, not the best friends or sidekicks of white protagonists. In *Scandal*, Kerry Washington plays a political operative. Washington became the first African-American lead to be nominated for an Emmy in 18 years. In *How to Get Away with Murder*, Viola Davis stars as law professor Annalise Keating. In 2015, Davis became the first black woman to win the Primetime Emmy Award for Outstanding Lead Actress in a Drama Series. Rhimes and others have shown how the power to create stories about women of color by women of color can result in multidimensional characters who are not afraid to be angry, complicated, and powerful.

## HERE WE ARE!

Globalization and its effects, both positive and negative, have made the world even more interconnected. The cheap goods bought in the United States may have been made by women facing violence in Mexico or girls in slavery in India.

Solidarity in the struggle for justice inspired *Sisterhood Is Global: The International Women's Movement Anthology*, a groundbreaking anthology published in 1984. Feminist Robin Morgan edited this collection of short essays from 70 countries. Many of the contributors had to remain anonymous, such as the writer from Haiti, because they were facing danger and persecution in their own countries.

It is now a classic, crossing cultural, racial, class, geographic, and ideological boundaries to understand the condition of women throughout the world. It examines significant factors in the lives of women, including life expectancy, the use of contraception and abortion, violence against women, and women's religious, secular, educational, and employment rights.

## SOLIDARITY, ENGAGEMENT, EMPOWERMENT

One way to understand the importance of an intersectional, transnational feminism for women of color is by using the concepts of solidarity, engagement, and empowerment. Solidarity is the foundation for social movements, as the 2017 Women's March on Washington organizers discovered when they encountered resistance from women of color to the lack of diversity in their leadership and the issues they planned to address. Engagement means not only understanding the multiple layers of oppression faced by many women of color but

## THE FUTURE IS CALLING

By 2050, women of color are projected to be the majority of all women in the United States. According to population projections from the US Census Bureau:

- White non-Hispanic women will be 47.5 percent of the total female population

- Hispanic or Latina will be 25.8 percent

- African American will be 13.1 percent

- Asian will be 8.7 percent[3]

These figures may not adequately reflect the increasing number of mixed-race or biracial women and others who choose not to identify themselves within these categories. The Census Bureau projects that women of color will make up approximately 53 percent of the female population by 2050.[4] In any case, women of color will no longer be "minority" women, and they will continue to make their voices heard.

becoming actively involved in ways of dismantling them. It is one of the most important ways of connecting the local with the global through civic engagement. Empowerment is what can happen when people act in solidarity and become engaged with their communities, whether in person or virtually, to work for equity and social justice.

Recommendations for specific change have included making sure that job creation is inclusive so that unemployed women of color and those in low-paying jobs can improve their economic security. Instead of more jobs, activists argue that the focus should be on better jobs that provide paid family medical leave, sick leave, and a living wage. Discrimination faced by older women of color should be brought to light and challenged. Women of color are often the primary caregivers in their families, and access to affordable childcare and health care is critical.

It should be clear that even though not all women of color are the same, many of the same factors have an impact on their lives. Gendered racism will not vanish overnight. But injustice can be challenged. Abolitionists saw slavery abolished. Suffragists saw women gain the vote. Civil rights workers saw segregation outlawed. The women's movement has seen progress on many fronts. For women of color, the future also holds the promise of change. In the words of Adichie, positive social change happens when "we begin to dream about and plan for a different world, a fairer world, a world of happier men and happier women who are truer to themselves."[5] Women of color play an important part in helping make this dream a reality: a better world for us all.

# DISCUSSION STARTERS

- Can you think of a representation of a woman of color in popular culture that turns expectations upside down? If so, how is this achieved?

- What roles do literature, film, and other art forms play in your life? What roles can they play in social change?

- In what ways can women of color help lead the way in improving life for all Americans?

# ESSENTIAL FACTS

## SIGNIFICANT EVENTS

- In 1851, Sojourner Truth addressed a women's rights convention in Akron, Ohio. During her speech, "Ain't I a Woman?," she challenged the gender and racial hierarchies faced by black women.

- In 1977, the term *women of color* was coined at the National Women's Conference to create solidarity and to make these women's specific concerns heard.

- Beginning in the 1980s, key scholars developed the concept of intersectionality. This is a way of describing the multiple layers of oppression brought about by race, gender, class, and sexuality.

- The Women's March was a worldwide protest held on January 21, 2017, the day after the inauguration of President Donald Trump.

## KEY PLAYERS

- Major women of color in early American social movements such as abolition and suffrage include Harriet Tubman, Sojourner Truth, and Mary Church Terrell. Later civil rights activists such as Septima Clark and Fannie Lou Hamer battled for the right to vote.

- Major women of color in the civil rights movement and subsequent movements include Rosa Parks, Elizabeth Eckford, Dolores Huerta, Sonia Sotomayor, and Lorelei DeCora Means.

- Kimberlé Crenshaw developed the concept of intersectionality in the 1980s.

- Alicia Garza, Patrisse Cullors, and Opal Tometi founded Black Lives Matter in 2013 to address inequity for people of color.

## IMPACT ON SOCIETY

As a result of systematic and institutional discrimination in many areas, women of color have suffered widening gaps compared to white women and to men of color. Women of color have been significantly impacted in what kinds of jobs they can get, what they are paid in contrast to white women and men of color, what access to health care they receive, how vulnerable they are to violence and trafficking, and how often they die of preventable causes. Gendered racism, stereotypes, and microaggressions can lead to chronic stress and the diseases related to it, such as heart disease and diabetes. These alarming disparities in pay, health care, safety, and leadership opportunities are still formidable barriers. Intersectionality calls for a broader way of addressing the multiple challenges of social justice so that equity of opportunity can become a reality for all.

## QUOTE

"Much feminist thought by individual visionary women of color (especially black women thinkers) and white female allies called for a more accurate representation of female identity, one that would consider the reality of intersectionality. This theory encouraged women to see race and class as well as gender as crucial factors shaping female destiny."

—*bell hooks, feminist and cultural critic*

# GLOSSARY

## EQUITY

Justice in the way people are treated, which does not mean treating people the same.

## FEMINISM

The belief that women should have the same opportunities and rights as men politically, socially, and economically.

## GENDER-BASED VIOLENCE

Violence by males against girls and women, including rape, sexual assault, stalking, and sexual harassment.

## GENDERED RACISM

A form of oppression faced by many women of color based on both race and gender.

## GLOBALIZATION

The movement toward a world more connected by trade, finance, and communications.

## HUMAN TRAFFICKING

A form of modern-day slavery that involves the trade and purchase of human beings for exploitation in forced labor and sexual slavery.

## INTERSECTIONALITY

Overlapping forms of oppression based on race, gender, class, sexuality, and other factors.

## LIVING WAGE

The minimum income necessary for a person to meet basic needs. Not the same as the minimum wage, which varies from state to state and is lower than a living wage.

## MICROAGGRESSION

A brief and commonplace daily behavior or speech that communicates negative bias to the target person or group.

## MISOGYNY

Hatred of or contempt for women.

## PATRIARCHY

A system of beliefs that empowers men at the expense of women.

## TRANSNATIONAL FEMINISM

An intersectional feminism concerned with how globalization and capitalism across cultures affect the condition of girls and women, especially women of color.

## WAGE GAP

For women of color, a phenomenon that includes both the gender pay gap, which is the average difference between what men and women are paid, and also the gap between what men of color and women of color are paid.

# ADDITIONAL
# RESOURCES

## SELECTED BIBLIOGRAPHY

Collins, Patricia Hill. *Black Feminist Thought*. New York: Routledge, 2000. Print.

Rojas, Maythee. *Women of Color and Feminism*. Berkeley, CA: Seal, 2009. Print.

## FURTHER READINGS

Edwards, Sue Bradford. *What Are Race and Racism?* Minneapolis, MN: Abdo, 2017. Print.

Jensen, Kelly, ed. *Here We Are: Feminism for the Real World*. Chapel Hill, NC: Algonquin, 2017. Print.

Thomas, Angie. *The Hate U Give*. New York: Balzer & Bray, 2017. Print.

## ONLINE RESOURCES

**Booklinks**
NONFICTION NETWORK
FREE! ONLINE NONFICTION RESOURCES

To learn more about sexism and race, visit **abdobooklinks.com**. These links are routinely monitored and updated to provide the most current information available.

# MORE INFORMATION

For more information on this subject, contact or visit the following organizations:

**THE NATIONAL WOMEN'S HISTORY MUSEUM**
205 S. Whiting Street Suite 254
Alexandria, VA 22304
703-461-1920
nwhm.org

The National Women's History Museum was founded in 1996 to tell the stories of women who have traditionally remained hidden in history. Its website features extensive online exhibitions on women of color, from precolonial information to black women in social movements to the history of Chinese women in American society and in film.

**THE SMITHSONIAN NATIONAL MUSEUM OF AFRICAN AMERICAN HISTORY AND CULTURE**
1400 Constitution Avenue NW
Washington, DC 20560
844-750-3012
nmaahc.si.edu

The National Museum of African American History and Culture was opened with much fanfare in September 2016 in a ceremony led by President Barack Obama. It is located on the National Mall in Washington, DC.

# SOURCE NOTES

## CHAPTER 1. THE MARCH HEARD AROUND THE WORLD

1. Barb Darrow. "Turns Out Attendance at Women's March Events Was Bigger Than Estimated." *Fortune*. Fortune, 23 Jan. 2017. Web. 17 Aug. 2017.

2. Kaveh Wadell. "The Exhausting Work of Tallying America's Largest Protest." *Atlantic*. Atlantic, 23 Jan. 2017. Web. 17 Aug. 2017.

3. Charlotte Krol. "Women's March: The Numbers behind the Global Rallies." *Telegraph*. Telegraph, 23 Jan. 2017. Web. 17 Aug. 2017.

4. Emily Tamkin and Robbie Gramer. "The Women's March Heard Round the World." *Foreign Policy*. Foreign Policy, 21 Jan. 2017. Web. 17 Aug. 2017.

5. Kimberlé Crenshaw. "Why Intersectionality Can't Wait." *Washington Post*. Washington Post, 24 Sept. 2015. Web. 17 Aug. 2017.

6. Michael Janofsky. "At Million Woman March, Focus Is on Family." *New York Times*. New York Times, 26 Oct. 1997. Web. 17 Aug. 2017.

7. Jia Tolentino. "The Somehow Controversial Women's March on Washington." *New Yorker*. New Yorker, 18 Jan. 2017. Web. 17 Aug. 2017.

8. Peggy McIntosh. "White Privilege: Unpacking the Invisible Knapsack." *Independent School* 49.2 (1990): 31. Web. 17 Aug. 2017.

9. Farah Stockman. "Women's March on Washington Opens Contentious Dialogues about Race." *New York Times*. New York Times, 9 Jan. 2017. Web. 17 Aug. 2017.

## CHAPTER 2. INVISIBLE SOLDIERS

1. "Modern History Sourcebook: Sojourner Truth: Ain't I a Woman?" *Fordham University*. Fordham University, 1997. Web. 17 Aug. 2017.

2. "7 Facts about Dolores Huerta." *Biography*. Biography, n.d. Web. 6 June 2017.

3. Stephanie Kirchner. "A House without a Home." *Washington Post*. Washington Post, 10 Apr. 2017. Web. 17 Aug. 2017.

4. Andrea Smith. "Native American Feminism, Sovereignty, and Social Change." *Feminist Studies* 31.1 (2005): 117. Web. 17 Aug. 2017.

## CHAPTER 3. SPEAKING UP, FIGHTING BACK

1. Judith K. Witherow. "Conquest: Sexual Violence and American Indian Genocide." *Off Our Backs* 35.11/12 (2005): 48. Print.

2. Jamaal Bell. "Race and Human Trafficking in the US: Unclear but Undeniable." *Huffington Post*. Huffington Post, 25 May 2011. Web. 17 Aug. 2017.

3. Priscilla Alvarez. "When Sex Trafficking Goes Unnoticed in America." *Atlantic*. Atlantic, 23 Feb. 2016. Web. 5 June 2017.

4. "Chinese American Women." *National Women's History Museum*. National Women's History Museum, 2008. Web. 5 June 2017.

5. "Domestic Violence among Latin@a." *National Latin@ Network*. National Latin@ Network, n.d. Web. 5 June 2017.

6. Alastair Leithead. "Boko Haram Abductions: Freed 'Bride' Tells of Stigma Ordeal." *BBC News*. BBC, 14 Apr. 2016. Web. 5 June 2017.

7. Gregg Zoroya. "'Honor Killings': 5 Things to Know." *USA Today*. USA Today, 9 June 2016. Web. 17 Aug. 2017.

8. Sam Ruland. "Former NFL Player Don McPherson Addresses Narrowed View of Masculinity." *Penn State Daily Collegian*. Penn State, 3 Mar. 2015. Web. 17 Aug. 2017.

9. Mitch Smith. "In Court, Diamond Reynolds Recounts Moments before a Police Shooting." *New York Times*. New York Times, 6 June 2017. Web. 17 Aug. 2017.

## CHAPTER 4. SILENT KILLERS

1. Mike Hixenbaugh. "Houston Doctors Determined to Reduce Cervical Cancer Deaths in Rio Grande Valley." *Houston Chronicle*. Houston Chronicle, 25 Nov. 2016. Web. 5 June 2017.

2. "Putting Women's Health Care Disparities on the Map." *Kaiser Family Foundation*. Kaiser Family Foundation, June 2009. Web. 5 June 2017.

3. Domenica Ghanem. "For Women of Color, the 'Healthcare Gap' Is Real and Deadly." *Hill*. Hill, 8 Mar. 2017. Web. 5 June 2017.

4. Lisa Margonelli. "Eternal Life." *New York Times*. New York Times, 7 Feb. 2010. Web. 16 June 2017.

5. "Women of Color Health Data Book." Office of Research on Women's Health. National Institutes of Health, 2014. Web. 12 Sept. 2017.

6. Jioni A. Lewis and Helen A. Neville. "Construction and Initial Validation of the Gendered Racial Microaggressions Scale for Black Women." *Journal of Counseling Psychology* 62.2 (Apr. 2015): 289–302. Web. 17 Aug. 2017.

## CHAPTER 5. THE LONGEST WALK

1. "Equity of Opportunity." *US Department of Education*. US Department of Education, 2017. Web. 5 June 2017.

2. Ivory A. Toldson. "The 'Acting White Theory' Doesn't Add Up." *Root*. Root, 30 Jan. 2013. Web. 17 Aug. 2017.

3. Ibid.

4. Anthony P. Carnevale, et al. "Recovery: Job Growth and Education Requirements through 2020." *Georgetown University Public Policy Institute*. Georgetown, 2014. Web. 17 Aug. 2017.

5. Barbara Gonzalez. "Sen. Rick Santorum Tells Dreamers to Go Back to Mexico." *Latina*. Latina, 8 Dec. 2016. Web. 17 Aug. 2017.

6. Ibid.

7. Farah Ahmad and Sarah Iverson. "The State of Women of Color in the United States." *Center for American Progress*. Center for American Progress, Oct. 2013. Web. 17 Aug. 2017.

8. Elizabeth Cohen. "Push to Achieve Tied to Suicide in Asian-American Women." *CNN International*. CNN, 16 May 2007. Web. 5 June 2017.

9. Edward Rodrigue and Richard V. Reeves. "Single Black Female BA Seeks Educated Husband: Race, Assortative Mating, and Inequality." *Brookings Institute*. Brookings Institute, 9 Apr. 2015. Web. 5 June 2017.

# SOURCE NOTES
## CONTINUED

## CHAPTER 6. WOMEN OF COLOR IN THE WORKFORCE

1. Adaku Onyeka-Crawford. "A Woman of Color Talks Poverty Data." *National Women's Law Center*. NWLC, 17 Sept. 2015. Web. 17 Aug. 2017.

2. Farah Ahmad and Sarah Iverson. "The State of Women of Color in the United States." *Center for American Progress*. Center for American Progress, Oct. 2013. Web. 17 Aug. 2017.

3. "Workplace Justice." *National Women's Law Center*. NWLC, Sept. 2016. Web. 11 July 2017.

4. Tanzina Vega. "The Steep Cost of Incarceration on Women of Color." *CNN Money*. CNN, 29 Nov. 2015. Web. 17 Aug. 2017.

5. Farah Ahmad and Sarah Iverson. "The State of Women of Color in the United States." *Center for American Progress*. Center for American Progress, Oct. 2013. Web. 17 Aug. 2017.

6. Asaf Levanon, Paula England, and Paul Allison. "Occupational Feminization and Pay: Assessing Causal Dynamics Using 1950–2000 US Census Data." *Social Forces*. Oxford Journals, Dec. 2009. Web. 17 Aug. 2017.

7. "Women of Color in the United States." *Knowledge Center*. Catalyst, 4 Feb. 2016. Web. 5 June 2017.

8. Jasmine Tucker and Caitlin Lowell. "National Snapshot: Poverty among Women & Families, 2015." *National Women's Law Center*. NWLC, Sept. 2016. Web. 17 Aug. 2017.

9. Farah Ahmad and Sarah Iverson. "The State of Women of Color in the United States." *Center for American Progress*. Center for American Progress, Oct. 2013. Web. 17 Aug. 2017.

10. Jasmine Tucker and Caitlin Lowell. "National Snapshot: Poverty among Women & Families, 2015." *National Women's Law Center*. NWLC, Sept. 2016. Web. 17 Aug. 2017.

11. Michael Grabell. "Exploitation and Abuse at the Chicken Plant." *New Yorker*. New Yorker, 8 May 2017. Web. 17 Aug. 2017.

## CHAPTER 7. LEANING IN, DIGGING DEEP

1. Mary C. Curtis. "Do Black Women Need Lessons on 'Leaning In?'" *Washington Post*. Washington Post, 25 Mar. 2013. Web. 17 Aug. 2017.

2. Susan T. Fiske. "Managing Ambivalent Prejudices: Smart-but-Cold and Warm-but-Dumb Stereotypes." *The Annals of the American Academy of Political and Social Science* 639 (2012): 33–48. Web. 17 Aug. 2017.

3. bell hooks. "Dig Deep: Beyond Lean In." *Feminist Wire*. Feminist Wire, 28 Oct. 2013. Web. 17 Aug. 2017.

4. Ibid.

5. Celisa Calacal. "Not a Single Black Woman Heads a Top Fortune 500 Company." *Alternet*. Alternet, 8 June 2017. Web. 17 Aug. 2017.

6. Derek Hawkins. "'Wise Latina Woman': Jeff Sessions, Race, and His Grilling of Sonia Sotomayor." *Washington Post*. Washington Post, 13 Jan. 2017. Web. 17 Aug. 2017.

7. Ibid.

8. Tom McCarthy. "Loretta Lynch Confirmed as US Attorney General after Delay 'to Spite Obama.'" *Guardian*. Guardian, 25 Apr. 2015. Web. 11 July 2017.

9. Susan T. Fiske. "Managing Ambivalent Prejudices: Smart-but-Cold and Warm-but-Dumb Stereotypes." *The Annals of the American Academy of Political and Social Science* 639 (2012): 33–48. Web. 17 Aug. 2017.

10. Farah Ahmad and Sarah Iverson. "The State of Women of Color in the United States." *Center for American Progress*. Center for American Progress, Oct. 2013. Web. 17 Aug. 2017.

11. Emily Peck. "Black Women Are Leaning In and Getting Nowhere: Ambitious Women Are Repeatedly Sidelined, a New Study Shows." *Huffington Post*. Huffington Post, 29 Sept. 2016. Web. 5 June 2017.

12. Ibid.

13. Farah Ahmad and Sarah Iverson. "The State of Women of Color in the United States." *Center for American Progress*. Center for American Progress, Oct. 2013. Web. 17 Aug. 2017.

14. "Facts and Figures: Leadership and Political Participation." *UN Women*. United Nations, n.d. Web. 17 Aug. 2017.

15. Ibid.

16. Annie Z. Yu. "Kamala Harris: The Women's March Is 'Absolutely Personal to Me.'" *Los Angeles Times*. 21 Jan. 2017. Web. 11 July 2017.

## CHAPTER 8. I DREAM A WORLD

1. Chimamanda Ngozi Adichie. "We Should All Be Feminists." *TED Talks*. TED, Apr. 2012. Web. 5 June 2017.

2. Zeba Blay. "When We Attack Serena Williams' Body, It's Really about Her Blackness." *Huffington Post*. Huffington Post, 9 Jan. 2017. Web. 17 Aug. 2017.

3. "Projections of the Population by Sex, Hispanic Origin, and Race for the United States: 2015 to 2060." *Population Projections*. US Census Bureau, 2014. Web. 17 Aug. 2017.

4. Ibid.

5. Chimamanda Ngozi Adichie. "We Should All Be Feminists." *TED Talks*. TED, Apr. 2012. Web. 5 June 2017.

# INDEX

# ABOUT THE AUTHORS

## DUCHESS HARRIS, JD, PHD

Professor Harris is the chair of the American Studies Department at Macalester College. The author and coauthor of four books (*Hidden Human Computers: The Black Women of NASA* and *Black Lives Matter* with Sue Bradford Edwards, *Racially Writing the Republic: Racists, Race Rebels, and Transformations of American Identity* with Bruce Baum, and *Black Feminist Politics from Kennedy to Clinton/Obama*), she has been an associate editor for *Litigation News*, the American Bar Association Section's quarterly flagship publication, and was the first editor-in-chief of *Law Raza Journal*, an interactive online race and the law journal for William Mitchell College of Law.

She has earned a PhD in American Studies from the University of Minnesota and a Juris Doctorate from William Mitchell College of Law.

## NADINE PINEDE, PHD

Nadine Pinede was born in Paris, France, of Haitian immigrants, and she has since lived in Canada, the United States, and Belgium. She holds degrees from Harvard and Oxford, where she was a Rhodes Scholar, and earned her PhD in Philosophy of Education. Her writing has appeared in numerous publications.